—Weird and Wacky Science—

KILLER ASTEROIDS

Margaret Poynter

ENSLOW PUBLISHERS, INC.

44 Fadem Road P.O. Box 38
Box 699 Aldershot
Springfield, N.J. 07081 Hants GU12 6BP
U.S.A. U.K.

Library of Congress Cataloging-in-Publication Data

Poynter, Margaret.
    Killer asteroids / Margaret Poynter.
       p. cm. — (Weird and wacky science)
    Includes bibliographical references and index.
    ISBN 0-89490-616-X
    1. Asteroids—Orbits—Juvenile literature. 2. Catastrophes (Geology)—Juvenile literature.
    [1. Asteroids. 2. Catastrophes (Geology)] I. Title. II. Series.
    QB377.P69 1996
    523.5—dc20   94-49124
                                                          CIP
                                                            AC

Printed in the United States of America

10 9 8 7 6 5 4 3 2

Illustration Credits: Department of Defense, p. 29; Hubble Space Telescope
Comet Team and NASA, pp. 34, 37, 40; Library of Congress, p. 22; NASA, pp.
4, 10, 15, 16, 18, 20; Courtesy of NASA, Jet Propulsion Laboratory, p. 32;
Courtesy of NASA, Jet Propulsion Laboratory, Steven Ostrow, pp. 26, 31; Palomar,
California Institute of Technology, p. 23; ©Jim Richardson/Westlight, p. 24;
United States Department of the Interior, National Park Service, p. 7; Public
Information Office, University of California, Berkeley, p. 13; H.A. Weaver, T.E.
Smith (Space Telescope Science Institute), and NASA, p. 38.

Cover Illustration: ©Lawrence Manning/Westlight

Contents

This painting shows an asteroid or comet slamming into tropical, shallow seas in what is now Mexico. Shown in the painting are pterodactyls, flying reptiles with wingspans of up to forty feet (12 meters), gliding above low, tropical clouds.

1
THE REIGN OF
THE DINOSAUR

They were here long before human beings existed. Some of them lived in hilly areas. Others thundered across the low plains. A few made their homes in dry deserts. Many more lived in lush forests. Still others spent their lives sloshing through swamps and large ponds. These largest and strongest of the world's creatures were found everywhere. For 140 million years, they ruled Earth.

They are now called dinosaurs, the "terrible lizards," though they were not lizards. Many of these reptiles were peaceful and harmless, not terrible. These creatures shared their world with other types of reptiles, and with insects, frogs, turtles, snails, and small mammals.

Dinosaurs came in many different shapes and sizes. Some

walked on all fours. Some were so heavy that they lived in swamps where the water could support their bodies. Still others stood on their hind legs, balanced by their tails.

There were dinosaurs that were only two feet long. One of the largest may have been 125 feet (38 meters) long. Some were as tall as a six-story building. It is believed that the heaviest dinosaur weighed more than fifty tons.[1]

Not all dinosaurs were carnivores—meat-eaters. Many of them were herbivores; they survived on diets of leaves and grass. The larger plant-eaters had to eat a ton of leaves a day to stay alive.

It used to be thought that all dinosaurs were cold-blooded creatures. They needed the sun to warm them up; otherwise, they were sluggish and slow-moving, like reptiles and amphibians today. Now it is thought that at least some of the dinosaurs were warm-blooded.[2] Like human beings, they produced their own heat when their muscles burned the food they ate. Such creatures could have been able to move as quickly as cats.

A Different World

The world of the dinosaurs was very different from the world of today. There were reptiles everywhere—on the land, in lakes, in the sea, and in the air. There were few very hot or very cold areas. In most places, the climate was warm and balmy. Great expanses of green jungles grew near the arctic circle.

At the beginning of the dinosaurs' reign all the earth's land was lumped together in one mass, dotted with small inland seas. There were no great oceans to interrupt the animals' movements. There were no towering mountain ranges to block their paths.

The earth's surface is made up of interlocking plates, which

Around 65 million years ago, dinosaurs disappeared. What caused the disappearance of the dinosaurs is still under debate.

are sections of land. These plates are always on the move. Because of this movement, the single land mass began to break up 150 million years ago. Huge chunks of land drifted away. Those pieces became the seven continents. Great mountain ranges rose when continents collided. The inland seas drained into the ocean. In some places the mild climate became cold.

In others it became much warmer. The average temperature rose by as much as twenty degrees. Some of the smaller creatures escaped the heat by creeping under brush and twigs. Others burrowed under clumps of weeds and grass.

The dinosaurs could do nothing to cool off. They had no sweat glands to release their body heat. When they panted, their mouths became parched. Those that found themselves in very hot, dry areas dragged their great weight to the nearest water hole. As time passed they found only dried mud. Some dinosaurs perished from the heat and lack of water.

Most dinosaurs were able to cope with their new environments. Their senses were keen, they were alert and aggressive, and they were adaptable. The world was changing, but the dinosaurs still ruled that world.

The Endless Night

Then, about 65 million years ago, catastrophe struck. In one area, there was a huge explosion. Dinosaurs grazing nearby were probably deafened by the sound. Tons of dust, ash, and soot filled the atmosphere. For six months the heat and light of the sun could not penetrate this dust cloud. The skies were dark, and the earth grew colder and colder. There were snowstorms.

Blundering about in the darkness, herbivores stripped the trees of every last leaf. Some of the hardier ones survived for a time by digging through the snow for grass and moss. They ate twigs and chewed the bark off dead trees. Eventually even that food supply was gone.

The carnivores continued to feast on their starving plant-eating cousins and helpless mammals. When there was no more prey, the ravenous creatures turned on each other. Cannibalism kept the strongest alive for a while longer.

As time passed the dust cloud began to disappear. Within ten years it was gone. By then the dinosaurs had become extinct. So had at least half the other species of plants and animals living on Earth. The course of evolution had been changed forever.

What caused the sudden, drastic events that led to the destruction of the dinosaurs? Could such a disaster ever occur again? To find the answers to those questions, scientists have looked for clues here on Earth.

They have also looked at outer space. Is there something out there that could destroy us as it destroyed the dinosaurs?

Many experts believe the answer to that question is "Yes."[3]

The Meteor Crater in Flagstaff, Arizona (top center), as seen from space. This photo was taken from the space station Skylab.

THE SEARCH
FOR CLUES

It was the morning of June 30, 1908. The Trans-Siberian Express was making its regular run across the plains of northern Russia. Its conductor was startled when he heard a series of loud bangs. *Has there been an accident?* he wondered.[1] After stopping the train, he rushed back to the passenger car. Here, a group of wide-eyed men and women said that they had heard the same noises—what sounded like explosions. Looking out the windows toward the source of the sounds, they had seen a bright blue ball of flame streaking across the sky. It had left a trail of smoke behind it.

Residents of the sparsely populated area had also seen and heard the explosion. Some of them lived near the 830 square miles (2,160 square kilometers) of forest that had been uprooted by the shock waves. Thirty miles (48 kilometers) away, others saw the bodies of the reindeer that had been killed by the blast. The tents of nomads camping several miles away were scattered. The clothes of a man who had been standing sixty miles (ninety-six kilometers) away caught on fire.

Because Russia was involved in wars and revolutions at this time, it was 1927 before scientists could safely travel to Siberia. Here they found the remains of the fallen forest. They saw small remnants of an object scattered over a wide area. There were also a number of small holes these remnants had made when they landed.

Many people have since tried to explain the mysterious event. Some say that an alien spaceship had exploded. Others say that a black hole had been bored into Earth and had come out in the Atlantic Ocean. Most experts have a more reasonable answer. They believe that a giant meteoroid, a piece of rocky or metallic space debris, had crashed onto the earth's surface.[2]

Now known as the Tunguska event, the blast had not occurred on the earth's surface. It had taken place five miles up in our atmosphere. It is now estimated that the explosion had the force of 12 million tons of TNT, a powerful explosive. It was eight hundred times more powerful than the force of the atomic bomb that leveled Hiroshima in 1945.

Bombardment from Space

Space debris has been falling on Earth for billions of years. It will continue falling as long as Earth exists. Each day, three or four twenty-pound meteoroids strike Earth's surface. Once every hundred years a 4,000-ton meteoroid falls from the sky, and once every 100,000 years a meteoroid weighing 50,000 tons or more plows into our small planet.

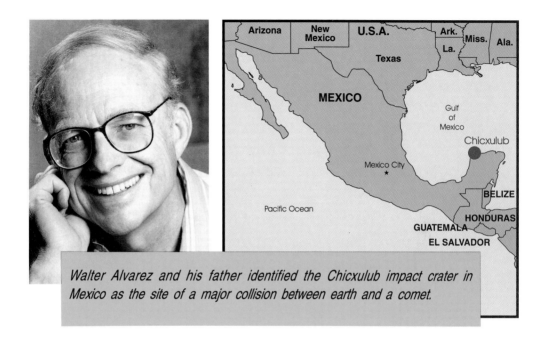

Walter Alvarez and his father identified the Chicxulub impact crater in Mexico as the site of a major collision between earth and a comet.

Earth's surface is scarred by at least 139 craters that resulted from collisions with large space objects. Only 50,000 years ago a 150-foot-wide (45 meters) iron asteroid smashed into what is now northern Arizona. At impact it was traveling about 25,000 miles (40,000 kilometers) per hour. The force of the collision sent 300 million tons of rock flying high into the air. It left a vast crater 660 feet deep (200 meters) and one mile (1.6 kilometers) wide. That crater could swallow a sixty-story building or hold eleven football fields.

Such a large object causes a lot of damage to the environment. Could a meteorite have led to the extinction of the dinosaurs? For many years, scientists tried to answer that question. In the late 1970s, Walter Alvarez, a geologist, was in Italy. He was studying a thin layer of clay that lay between two layers of rock. This same layer of clay exists in various parts of the world. The rock above the clay had been formed later than the rock below it. The clay marked the boundary between two geologic eras. A geologic era is a period of time in history. Each era is marked by distinctive types of rock and rock formations.

As Alvarez poked and pried into the bottom layer of rock, he found dinosaur fossils embedded in it. He then examined the upper layer of rock. Here there were no such fossils. That layer of clay must have been formed at the same time that the dinosaurs vanished.

Later other scientists studied samples of the same clay. One of them was Walter's father, Luis, a physicist. The team made an important and exciting discovery: There were traces of iridium in the clay. Iridium is a metal that is seldom found naturally on the earth's surface. It is, however, often found in meteorites.

A Doomsday Rock

Other geologic studies found iridium in the same layer of clay in other parts of the world. There were also bits of glassy rock called tektites, which are formed when asteroid debris mixes with superhot gases. These and other discoveries led to a startling conclusion: Sixty-five million years ago a one-hundred-ton meteoroid must have slammed into Earth. When the huge, fast-moving object plowed into the ground, there was a rapid release of energy.

That energy was converted into heat. Most of the meteorite vaporized; it changed into gas. The rocks close by the crash scene were also vaporized. The vapor expanded and exploded. The blast was 10,000 times more powerful than the combined explosions of all the nuclear weapons in the world today. It left a deep crater

This radar image shows the southwest portion of the buried Chicxulub impact crater in the Yucatán Peninsula, Mexico. The crater is about 190 miles (300 kilometers) in diameter and is buried in 1,000-3,300 feet (300-1,000 meters) of limestone.

in the ground. The dust and debris from the crater were thrown high into the atmosphere.

Does the crater caused by this doomsday rock still exist? Had it survived the eroding forces of wind and rain? Many experts believe they know the exact spot where the meteoroid crashed to Earth.[3] This spot is in what is now Mexico's Yucatán Peninsula. Here, a mile underground, there is a circular crater 190 miles (300 kilometers) wide. Scientific testing of rock samples taken from the rim of this mammoth hole shows that this rock was once melted, and then it hardened. These samples resembled volcanic rock, but the rock had not melted slowly, as volcanic rock does. These rocks had melted suddenly, as they would in an explosion.

Studies showed that this melted rock was formed 65 million years ago, when the layer of clay was formed. It was at this same time that the dinosaurs disappeared from Earth.

The comet Kohoutek was photographed from Skylab 4 on December 25, 1973. The tail is approximately 3 million miles (4.8 million kilometers) long.

3
LIFE IN THE FAST LANE

We still do not know the entire truth about the dinosaurs' disappearance. We do know that, at various times, other species have suddenly vanished. Some of those cases have also been linked to objects from space colliding with our planet.

It is not surprising that these collisions occur, because Earth is like a spaceship. Traveling 65,000 miles (104,000 kilometers) per hour, it makes continuous voyages around the Sun. Earth is not alone in its travels: Like a freeway during rush hour or a school hallway between class periods, the space in our solar system contains a lot of traffic. Whizzing past Earth in the same or the opposite direction there are specks of dust and grains of sand, pebbles, and small rocks, and boulders as large as trucks or houses.

Killer Asteroids

The asteroid belt lies between the orbits of Jupiter and Mars. Here, there are millions of asteroids orbiting around the sun.

Asteroids

In space there are also huge chunks of stone or metal; some are the size of mountains, others the size of small cities. The largest of these "flying mountains" is 600 miles (nearly 1,000 kilometers) in diameter. These miniature planets have craters from past impacts with other large objects.

Through a telescope these larger pieces of space rubble look like points of light. The ancient Greeks thought they were stars. Today, we call them asteroids, which is Greek for "starlike." Asteroids are leftovers from the creation of our solar system 4.5 million years ago. Some of them are parts of a planet that was never completed; some are pieces that were chipped off another asteroid during a collision. Some asteroids are made of rock; others have cores of dense metal. Some have smaller asteroids orbiting around them.

The asteroid belt lies between Mars and Jupiter, where there is plenty of room. Their orbits may remain stable for millions of years. Sometimes, though, two asteroids collide. In this game of cosmic billiards one of them gets knocked out of its orbit. Eventually it is caught by the gravity of a larger body. It may keep traveling in a shortened orbit, or it may collide with the larger body. Many of the craters on the moons and planets of our solar system are the result of collisions with asteroids.

Earth's gravity pulls a few asteroids into our planet's neighborhood. Currently there are more than one hundred known asteroids whose orbits cross Earth's orbit. An asteroid travels at ten to thirty miles (sixteen to forty-eight kilometers) a second. When a building-sized asteroid smacks into our atmosphere, friction heats it up to thousands of degrees. When it gets hot enough, it blows up with a blinding flash of light called a meteor.

From Earth, these meteors, or shooting stars, appear to be streaks of light across the night sky. The smaller meteors go *pffft* and disappear from view in the blink of an eye. The larger meteors look like fireballs. The remnants leave a blazing trail across the sky.

Mammoth fireballs can be created when asteroids explode. At such times powerful shock waves ripple through Earth's atmosphere. One such event took place high above Indonesia in 1988. The force of the explosion was calculated to be equal to that of 5,000 tons of high explosives. Seen from Earth, the meteor looked like a flash of light as bright as the sun.

On February 1, 1994, what may have been a 100-yard (90-meter) wide rocky asteroid exploded over the South Pacific. The force of the blast was equal to that of 110,000 tons of TNT. The explosion lit up the sky.

A meteorite in a dry nitrogen cabinet undergoes study in the meteorite processing lab at Johnson Space Center. This meteorite was discovered in 1981 by an Antarctic meteorite recovery team and is thought to be of Martian origin.

Comets

Comets begin in a region beyond Pluto called the Oort Cloud. At first, they look like tumbling dirty snowballs. The core is less than 10 miles (15 kilometers) across. At this stage, they are too far away to be seen from Earth.

Occasionally a group of young comets is snared by the gravity from a passing star. The comets then travel in an orbit that plunges them from their birthplace toward the sun. During this journey they pass by Jupiter or Saturn. The paths of some of the comets are changed by the gravity of these planets.

About once every century, a comet careens toward the inner solar system. Somewhere between Jupiter and Mars, the sun's heat turns the comet's frozen gases into vapor. The vapor, combined with particles of ice, streams out behind the comet's core, forming a tail.

Meanwhile, the core of the comet erupts with great puffs of gas and dust. Like the thrusters on a spacecraft, these puffs can nudge the comet into a different course. It may then enter our inner solar system.

Only a few such stragglers are ever seen from Earth. By that time they are very old comets. The warmth of the sun is causing them to come apart. Eventually all the ice melts. All that remains are the rock and dust that form the core. The comet then resembles an asteroid.

An entire mature comet can fill a space much larger than Earth. The cloud of hydrogen that surrounds the comet's core can be larger than the Sun. Despite its size, a comet has very little mass. This lack of mass means that it does not exert much gravitational pull. It passes closely to moons and planets without disturbing them.

This picture of Halley's Comet was taken just as a meteor streaked across the sky.

On the other hand, a comet can easily be pulled off course by a giant planet—Jupiter, Saturn, or Uranus. It then becomes locked into a shorter orbit and approaches the sun at regular intervals. With each approach, the sun's heat causes more of the comet's ice to melt. The more ice that melts, the shorter the comet's life span becomes.

About two hundred of these periodic comets visit Earth's cosmic neighborhood regularly. The most famous is Halley's Comet, which reappears every seventy-six to seventy-nine years. In 1910 astronomers predicted that Earth would pass through Halley's tail. Some scientists said that we would be exposed to toxic space gases. There was worldwide panic; people pushed and shoved to buy gas masks. Fortunately, the scientists were proved to be wrong.

Another periodic comet is called Swift-Tuttle. It was seen in 1862, then again spotted in September 1992. On November 7, 1992, it passed within 110 million miles (160 million kilometers) of Earth. Each August, Earth crosses Swift-Tuttle's orbit. Even though the comet itself is far away on its 130-year journey around the sun, the particles it left behind remain in orbit. When Earth crosses the orbit, the particles burn up in the atmosphere. From the ground, the burning particles appear to be streaks of light. This event is called the Perseid meteor shower. It is one of the most spectacular annual meteor showers.

It has been predicted that Swift-Tuttle will return to Earth's area of space on August 14, 2126. On that date, it will come much closer to our planet than it did in 1992. One astronomer figured it may come within 14 million miles (22 million kilometers) of Earth.[1] It will be moving at 130,000 miles (200,000 kilometers) per hour. There is no doubt that Swift-Tuttle's 2126 meteor shower will be one of the great sky shows of all time.

The Bayeux Tapestry captures the wonder of the people who saw a comet over Europe in 1066. Scientists believe this was one of Halley's Comet's periodic flyovers.

Astronomers use telescopes such as this one to observe the skies.

4

OUTWITTING A DOOMSDAY ROCK

It is estimated that Swift-Tuttle's core is five miles (eight kilometers) across. The dinosaurs' doomsday rock was probably about that size. What if Swift-Tuttle changes its course ever so slightly? What if its jets nudge it toward Earth during its next visit?

For a while astronomers thought that Earth might be in danger in 2126. Now they believe that Swift-Tuttle will not be a real threat until 3044.[1] If it strikes the earth's surface, so much dust will be thrown into our atmosphere that all crops will die. Many of the world's animals will perish. Very few human beings will survive. The survivors may have to live as our cave-dwelling ancestors lived. They will have to pick berries and dig roots. With luck, they will find a pig or a cow to eat.

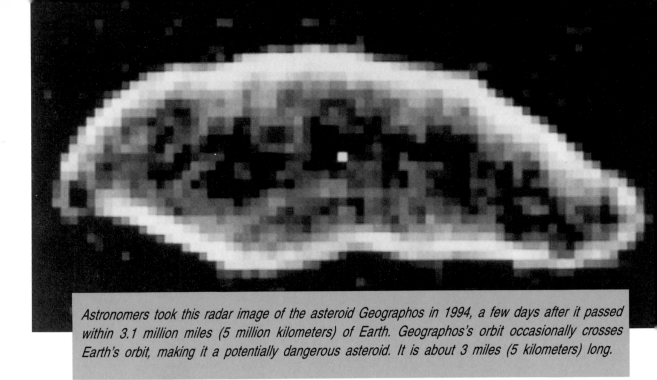

Astronomers took this radar image of the asteroid Geographos in 1994, a few days after it passed within 3.1 million miles (5 million kilometers) of Earth. Geographos's orbit occasionally crosses Earth's orbit, making it a potentially dangerous asteroid. It is about 3 miles (5 kilometers) long.

Swift-Tuttle could become Earth's doomsday rock; so could at least 128 asteroids whose orbits now cross that of our planet. On the average, an object two-thirds of a mile (one kilometer) wide will strike Earth once every 125,000 years. A 1.2-mile (2 kilometers) object will strike our planet once every million years.[2]

Our moon bears the scars of such collisions; so do the other planets and their moons. On Earth, however, it appears that those space objects did more than leave scars. It may have been a visiting comet that furnished the molecules needed for life to develop.[3] Our oceans may have been produced in part by a watery invader from outer space.

What about the dinosaurs' doomsday rock? Before it struck, many primitive mammals fell prey to giant predators. The extinction of the dinosaurs cleared the way for the mammals to thrive and develop, eventually leading to the appearance of the first human beings.

If those humans had had to share their planet with giant meat-eating reptiles, they would not have survived. The dinosaurs would still be ruling the earth.

Preventing the Final Disaster

Today it is unlikely that any good would come to Earth from being struck by a large comet or asteroid. So far such an object has not landed in a highly populated area, but what if the object that exploded over Siberia in 1908 had slammed into a large city? It could have destroyed hundreds of buildings. It could have killed tens of thousands of people.

Experts agree that sometime in the future, such an object could cause either a local or a worldwide catastrophe.[4] If nothing is done, human beings might go the way of the dinosaurs. The difference is that prehistoric creatures could not save themselves. They did not even know they were in danger.

Because of modern scientific knowledge, we are now very aware of the danger. The challenge is to use that knowledge to prevent what could be Earth's final disaster. The first step is to identify all possible doomsday rocks. Scientists are now studying old films of large asteroids to determine where those asteroids are now. In this way they can figure out their orbits.

There are also plans for a Project Spaceguard. This project will consist of six telescopes based at different sites around the world. The goal will be to locate any mountain-sized asteroid whose orbit crosses Earth's orbit. The telescopes will also locate any nearby comets.

When a possible doomsday rock is found, the next step is to determine when it will enter Earth's atmosphere. In July 1992 one asteroid was seen a dozen times. Scientists have a good idea of its orbit. Now they have to figure out its path around the sun. They will then know the asteroid's position for decades to come. They will be able to predict whether or not it is a danger to Earth.

Is it possible to ward off a threatening space object? There are many ideas about how to save the Earth from such an unwelcome visitor. Some involve the use of nuclear bombs; the people who like this idea hope that the bomb would blast the object just as our defensive weapons can now blast an incoming enemy rocket. The problem is that a comet or an asteroid is much further away than an enemy rocket. It is also moving much faster. A doomsday rock would be approaching Earth at 67,000 miles (100,000 kilometers) per hour.

Problems

What if we actually could bomb the threatening object? The bombs that now exist could deflect a smaller space object, but for a large asteroid the bomb might have to be ten thousand times more powerful than any that we have at this time. How would this weapon be delivered to the asteroid or the comet? An orbiting spacecraft loaded with such a cargo could be almost as dangerous as a killer rock from space would be. Perhaps a nuclear-tipped rocket could be used.

There is another problem with bombing a doomsday rock. An atomic blast might shatter it into tiny pieces, but it might break it up into several large pieces instead. What if these pieces all plowed into Earth's surface? Our planet might survive, but there would be a lot of damage. Many lives would probably be lost.

It has been suggested that we don't actually have to bomb a

Some people have proposed that ICBMs (Intercontinental Ballistic Missiles) could be sent into space to destroy oncoming comets and asteroids.

doomsday rock. A nuclear bomb could be detonated miles away from the object. The shock waves from the explosion would nudge the object off its threatening course. A gentle push of only a few hundred feet would do the job. Over millions of miles that short distance would be magnified. Earth would be saved.

A comet's course could also be changed if it were hit with a huge heating device. The quickly melting ice would cause more jets of steam. Those jets might steer the comet away from Earth, but they also might speed up the comet's journey *toward* our planet.

Some people are concerned that the storage and use of super bombs would be almost as dangerous as a killer rock from space. They are worried that one of them might be set off accidentally or would explode too soon. They say that the radiation from a nuclear explosion in space may put our planet in peril.

Scientists reply that there would be no more danger from super bombs than from the nuclear weapons that already exist. All such weapons are surrounded by security and have built-in safeguards to prevent any accidents. Their direction and time of detonation can be precisely controlled. A weapon directed at a doomsday rock would be detonated millions of miles from Earth. At that distance, the radiation would do us no harm.

Still, the use of nuclear weapons is enough of a worry to cause some experts to search for other methods of dealing with killer rocks from space. They suggest that a solar sail could deflect a dangerous comet. This device would catch the charged particles that stream from the sun and affect a comet's orbit. Their capture by the sail would cause the comet's path to be changed.

An orbiting mirror could focus a tight beam of sunlight on a threatening asteroid. The ray would vaporize part of the asteroid's surface. A jet of dust and ash would be created. Over months or years that jet could shove the asteroid away from Earth. Another idea would be to use the space shuttle to place a shield in orbit around our planet.

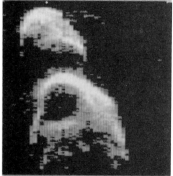

Other scientists suggest using antimatter to deflect the killer rock.[5] All mass is composed of very small particles of matter. Each of these particles has a corresponding particle of antimatter. When matter meets antimatter, they both self-destruct in a *poof* of pure energy. No one knows how the antimatter could be delivered to the space object, though. Since a rocket is made of matter, it would be destroyed as soon as the antimatter cargo was loaded.

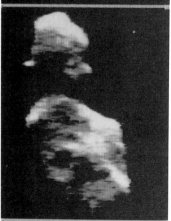

Playing the Odds

There is no shortage of ideas about how to deal with a killer rock from space. All of them would be very expensive. We have limited amounts of money and resources.

The asteroid Toutatis is actuallly two separate pieces of rock; one is about 1.6 miles (2.5 kilometers) in diameter and the other is about 0.9 miles (1.5 kilometers) in diameter. Scientists predicted that Toutatis would pass within 3.3 million miles (5.3 million kilometers) of Earth in 1996.

Asteroid Ida is so large it has its own moon, the tiny white dot to the right of the asteroid. Ida is 35 miles (55 kilometers) across.

During one human lifetime, there is a one in twenty thousand chance that a mountain-sized rock will crash into Earth. During that same lifetime, a person may be killed in a car accident or be infected with a fatal disease. An 8.0 earthquake could destroy an entire city. Should we spend our money to improve driver safety or to find a cure for the disease or to find a way to predict earthquakes? Or should we spend it to outwit a killer rock from space?

Dangerous asteroids and comets are out there. Someday one of them will be on a collision course with Earth. Perhaps for now we should just watch the skies. Programs such as Project Spaceguard do not cost much. They could help scientists discover a doomsday rock early enough to prepare a defense.

Human beings may yet meet the same fate as that of the dinosaurs, but we may not. We are the only species that is aware of the danger. We are the only species that should be able to do something about it.

The segments of Shoemaker-Levy 9 were called a "string of pearls" approaching Jupiter.

THE GREATEST SHOW
IN OUTER SPACE

The comet was formed as our solar system was being formed. For 4.5 billion years it traced a path through outer space. Then the sun nudged it off its usual course. Fifty years ago it was caught in the pull of Jupiter's gravity. Each time it orbited the planet it was drawn deeper into the Jovian atmosphere. In 1992, the force of the planet's gravity started ripping apart the icy dust ball. The glowing string of fragments continued to orbit Jupiter.

In March 1994, astronomers Carolyn and Eugene Shoemaker and David Levy spotted a long, fuzzy-looking object in outer space. They identified the object as a comet, and it became known as comet Shoemaker-Levy 9. At the time of discovery, Shoemaker-Levy 9 consisted of twenty-one large pieces and thousands of smaller ones. They were approaching the far side of

Jupiter, the side that always faces away from Earth. All the larger pieces were on a collision course with the planet. It was predicted that the first fragment would plunge onto Jupiter's gaseous surface on July 16, 1994.

Jupiter is two and a half times larger than all the other planets combined. More than thirteen hundred Earths could be packed inside it. Astronomers believed that the large body could easily survive the blows of the comet fragments.

They did not know what either the immediate or the long-term effects of the pummeling would be. By the spring of 1994, hundreds of telescopes on Earth were focused on the shattered comet. Cameras on board two spacecraft were set to take pictures of the collision.

Pummeling Jupiter

On Saturday, July 16—right on schedule—the first fragment crashed onto Jupiter. The mountain-sized clump created a fireball half the size of Earth. The bubble of superheated gas was brighter than anything else on Jupiter. It was brighter than Io, its brightest moon.

By Sunday evening, seven fragments had blasted through the planet's whirling cloud cover. They were traveling at more than 130,000 miles (200,000 kilometers) per hour, sixty times faster than the speed of a bullet. The rock-hard chunks of ice and dust had built up a tremendous energy of motion. When they hit Jupiter's wispy cloud cover, friction stopped them dead.

The smallest piece was only a half-mile wide, but it exploded with the force of 10 million megatons of TNT. It left a spreading plume of hot gas and debris as large as the earth itself. Such a collision would

An artist drew this view of Shoemaker-Levy 9 as it approached Jupiter.

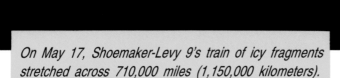

On May 17, Shoemaker-Levy 9's train of icy fragments stretched across 710,000 miles (1,150,000 kilometers).

vaporize the city of Los Angeles in an instant. It would be the worst natural disaster ever experienced by human beings.

Each impact produced a mammoth fireball. The temperature at their centers was at least 53,000°F (26,000°C). The impacts left huge black scars on Jupiter's backside. The heat was so intense that the atmosphere was speckled with pieces of fried debris. Fiery plumes shot up hundreds of miles. The flames edged over Jupiter's horizon, where they became visible to telescopes on Earth.

On Monday morning, a two-mile-wide fragment streaked sixty miles (one hundred kilometers) into Jupiter's atmosphere. Its blast was hundreds of times more powerful than the combined energy of all of Earth's nuclear weapons. The fireball it created spewed 1,300 miles (2,000 kilometers) into space. It was fifty times more luminous than Jupiter itself—so bright that, for a moment, it blinded the largest telescopes on Earth.

That collision gave Jupiter a "black eye" 9,600 miles (15,000 kilometers) across. The impact site was twice as large as Earth.

Two more fragments struck on Tuesday. The white-hot glow created by one of them was three times the size of Earth. By now raging storms were ripping through Jupiter's atmosphere. On Wednesday, five more pieces of the dying comet added to the turbulence. They stirred up the brimstone soup of sulfur, ammonia, hydrogen, and helium. As David Levy remarked, "Jupiter has had the stuffing knocked out of it."[1]

Thursday saw the explosions of four mountain-sized fragments. They created overlapping fireballs at ten-hour intervals. The blackened impact sites were so close that they almost merged into each other.

The final large fragment struck after midnight, adding its plume to the ring of swirling, superheated gas. The comet was now completely destroyed, and, as predicted, the planet Jupiter had survived the battering.[2]

The spectacular cosmic show lasted only a few days, but what we learn from Shoemaker-Levy 9 will last forever. "The best way to find out about something is to poke it and see what happens," said one astronomer. "We just gave the atmosphere of Jupiter a giant poke."

A Chance to Learn

Most scientists used to believe that Earth had been formed by a series of gradual changes. Then they saw the neatly arranged rows of craters on two of Jupiter's moons, and the random scattering of craters on our own moon. Now, for the first time, human beings had seen how these

Shoemaker-Levy 9 left several impact scars on the planet Jupiter.

craters were formed. It was clear that the bodies in our solar system were shaped largely by stupendous explosions.

What we can learn from Shoemaker-Levy 9 goes far beyond Jupiter itself. Perhaps we will get a better idea of how comets formed our own planet, how comets brought water to Earth, or how they brought life to Earth. The knowledge that we gain will help us better understand our entire solar system. It could give us the key to unlock some of the secrets of the universe.

Chapter 1

1. Lawrence Pringle, *Dinosaurs and Their World* (New York: Harcourt Brace, 1968), p. 38.

2. William Stout, *The Dinosaurs* (New York: Bantam Books, 1981), p. 4.

3. Carl Zimmer, "The Smoking Crater," *Discover*, January 1992, p. 48.

Chapter 2

1. Nigel Calder, *The Comet is Coming* (New York: Penguin Books, 1980), p. 124.

2. Ibid., p. 125.

3. Carl Zimmer, "The Smoking Crater," *Discover*, January 1992, p. 46.

Notes by Chapter

Chapter 3

1. David H. Levy, *The Quest for Comets* (New York: Plenum Press, 1994), p. 7.

Chapter 4

1. David H. Levy, *The Quest for Comets* (New York: Plenum Press, 1994), pp. 10–11.

2. "Doomsday Science," *Newsweek*, November 23, 1992, p. 60.

3. Levy, p. 216.

4. Ibid.

5. "Vision for the 21st Century", *Ad Astra*, June 1990, pp. 26–29.

Chapter 5

1. Sharon Begley and Mary Hager, "Good Show, by Jove," *Newsweek*, August 1, 1994, p. 60.

2. Ibid., p. 62.

asteroid—A small planetlike object in space. Thousands of asteroids orbit around the sun in the asteroid belt, which lies between Mars and Jupiter.

atmosphere—The mass of air surrounding Earth.

carnivore—An animal that eats other animals.

comet—A space object composed of ice and dust.

extinct—No longer existing; used to describe species of plants or animals that have disappeared.

Glossary

fossil—Any trace of an extinct plant or animal that has been preserved in the Earth's crust.

herbivore—An animal that eats only plants.

iridium—A metal found in meteorites.

Jovian—Having to do with the planet Jupiter.

megaton—A million tons.

meteor—A flaming space object.

meteorite—A stone or metallic object that has fallen to Earth from space.

meteoroid—A solid object in the solar system left over from the formation of the universe.

meteor shower—A swarm of meteors.

tektite—A glassy rounded object formed in the sudden heat and release of gases. Volcanic eruptions and meteors crashing to the earth are events where tektites are formed.

NEAR-EARTH OBJECTS

The following is a list of near-Earth objects (NEOs) with their distance from Earth at closest approach. There are more than 300 known NEOS.

DESIGNATION	NUMBER	DIAM. (km)	DIST. (AU)	DATE
1989 AC Toutatis	4179	5	0.0354	12/25/1996
1974 MA*		5		
1992 CC1		4	0.1367	9/15/2004
1994 AH2		3	0.1930	6/17/1998
1993 WD		2	0.2102	11/23/1995
1993 VW		2	0.0862	4/24/2004
1992 QN		2	0.1588	1/18/1996
1992 JE		2	0.2480	8/2/2005
1991 VK		2	0.0749	1/10/1997
1991 BB		2	0.1662	7/27/2000
1992 TA	4197	2	0.0846	10/25/1996
1992 FE	5604	1	0.0768	6/22/2002
1990 SP	5645	1	0.2295	12/27/2001
1990 SM		1	0.0747	2/17//2003
1989 VA		<1	0.2421	10/24/2003

Designation=The designation is provisional.

Diam.(km)=Diameter in kilometers (km). One kilometer is approximately 1.609 miles. To figure out the diameter in miles, multiply the number of kilometers by 0.621.

Dist.(AU)=Distance in astronomical units (AU). Since distances in space are so great, astronomers use this measurement. One AU is approximately 93 million miles. To figure out the distance the NEO will be from Earth, multiply the AUs by 93,000,000.

Date=Close Approach Date, or the date the object will be nearest to Earth. Astronomers have actually been able to calculate the time of the approach to the nearest second.

*This object has been lost. No data beyond the approximate size are known.

Exploring Space: From Ancient Legends to the Telescope to Modern Space Missions. New York: Scholastic, 1994.

Gallant, Roy A. *Macmillan Book of Astronomy.* New York: Macmillan Children's Book Group, 1986.

Further Reading

Lancaster-Brown, Peter. *Skywatch: Eyes-on Activities for Getting to Know the Stars, Planets & Galaxies.* New York: Sterling Publishing Company, 1993.

Levy, D. H. *The Quest for Comets: An Explosive Trail of Beauty & Danger.* New York: Plenum Publishing Corporation, 1994.

Nardo, Don. *The Extinction of the Dinosaurs.* San Diego: Lucent Books, 1994.

Schwartz, Jacob. *Asteroid Name Encyclopedia.* St. Paul, Minn.: Llewellyn Publications, 1995.

Index

J

Jupiter
   comets' journey to, 21, 35
   effect on comets, 22
   hit by comet fragment, 35–41
   impact sites, 39

L

Levy, David, 35, 39
Los Angeles, 38

M

Mars, 21
meteor, 19
meteorite, 13, 14, *20*
meteoroid, 12, 14
meteor shower, 23

N

nuclear bomb, 12, 14, 28, 30

O

Oort Cloud, 21

P

periodic comets, 22–23
Pluto, 21
Project Spaceguard, 27, 33

R

Russia, 11, 12

S

Saturn, 21, 22
Siberia, 12, 27
Shoemaker, Carolyn, 35
Shoemaker, Eugene, 35
Shoemaker-Levy 9, 35, 39, 41
Skylab, *10, 16*
solar sail, 30
South Pacific, 19
Swift-Tuttle, 23, 25, 26
   frequency of, 23
   speed of, 23
   threat to Earth, 25

T

tektites, 14
Trans-Siberian Express, 11
Tunguska event, 11–12

U

Uranus, 22

V

volcanic rock, 15

Y

Yucatán Peninsula, 15